Would I Have Sexted Back in the 80s?

"There is no clear cultural psyche for parenting digital teens. It is time we created one and brought some etiquette into our online world."

Allison Ochs

Would I Have Sexted Back in the 80s?

A Modern Guide to Parenting Digital Teens,
Derived from Lessons of the Past

Allison Ochs

Mark, I hope this makes you smile.

[signature]

AUP

\

Cover design: Ricardo Rivera & Corinne Guy

Illustrations by the talented 18-year-old Ricardo Rivera
Lay-out: Crius Group, Hulshout

ISBN   9789463721912
e-ISBN   9789048544219
NUR   854

To Markus, Carli, Moses, and Maya. And of course, to Mom, Dad and my ten siblings. I could not have written this book without you. I love you all.

A note from the author

I know you are possibly busy and tired. I get it, and this book was set up just for you. Talking to parents around the world, I have come to realize that parents don't want another academic book about raising a digital teen. What they want and need is hands-on advice. It should be short, simple, sweet, and to the point.

This book was set up with sections on topics that concern parents today. Feel free to browse, skip sections, and read whatever you need. If your child doesn't game – skip that section.

If you do, however, read the entire book and notice something is coming up in more than one section, it means I think this is extremely important. Important enough to repeat time and time again, making sure that whoever picks up this book will find that advice.

Contents

Introduction

After a long day of presenting to teens about sexting, porn, relationships, and dating, I headed home. The radio was blaring in my car and an 80s song came on. Just at that moment, I started thinking of how things have changed since my teen years and about the boy I had a crush on.

I had to ask myself this question: Would I have? As I pondered, I found my mind wandering back to 1986, the music in the car helping me. Man, oh man was the boy I liked a looker! I saw him smile at me from across the hallway. He was wearing his letterman jacket; that was it... I was a goner.

I flirted, smiled, and did just about anything I could to get his attention. The amount of time I spent on my wardrobe during those months was insane. I was making some progress, he had taken note of me, he knew my name and talked to me.

I decided to join the indoor track team, for no other reason than to be close to him, he was on the team. That way I would see him at training. I wasn't very talented, had no chance of winning, but no matter, off to track I went, where I swooned over him as he bolted by me.

An out-of-state meet approached, and the only way I could go was to run the 400 meters. This was not what I did; I was a high jumper. I hated running and feared being humiliated, losing, falling on my face, but nevertheless, I told my coach, "Sure I'll run. I'll train and be just fine."

Why did I do such a stupid thing? That is a very easy question to answer... He was going, my heartthrob was going to go, and if I went it would mean I could possibly sit with him on the ride up to Boise, Idaho.

Not only did I go, but I also maneuvered my way into the car he was in. As we drove up I-15 direction Idaho, I sat in the front seat, he was directly behind me. The music was blaring some 80s hits, we were laughing, and he was playing with my hair, stroking it and talking softly. When we arrived at the hotel he asked me if I was coming to the pool. I quickly put my suit on and floated in the water with him. I was interested, excited, and giddy, so was he... Still, nothing happened.

The competition for this particular boy was fierce. He was a football player and good at it. What's more, his dad had been to Harvard – all the parents and other kids whispered about how he was not only athletic but smart like his dad. Everyone knew this magical boy, with his blond, slightly curled hair and quiet charm, was a good catch; a high-school girl's dream was wrapped up in this one particular boy.

I was not alone in my pursuit of him; he was playing the field before he decided who would have the 'honor' of being his girl. I knew I was in the running, almost there, but one other girl was in the race with me and giving it her all.

One Friday night, after a stomp (a dance after a game in the school gym) he walked over to me, "Can I drive you home?" Of course I accepted. He was shy, I was shy, and there we sat, parked in front of my house, talking. It was electric. I could feel his body leaning in; I could feel his fear. He wanted to kiss me, I wanted him to kiss me, and I thought, "Could he possibly not know that I would do anything for him right now?" I was about to win; he was falling towards me, talking softly about school, nudging ever closer to kiss me. My heart was racing by now. I had never been kissed and to have a boy a year older kiss me, want me... And then, before he reached me, out of the blue there was a loud banging at the window of his car with an even more booming voice, "Yo dude, my sister needs to come in now. Ali, come on it's late." I stammered a "bye" and walked in.

I knew that was it. The other girl was his girlfriend by the end of the next week. My brothers, one in particular, scared him off. I have never forgotten.

Do you remember? I think we all remember that first love, that first flirt, and how scared we were. I lost that night. Having big brothers was a drag sometimes, especially when it came to my relationships with boys – but they sure kept me safe. They talked to me about boys, about locker-room talk and about what 'boys' wanted. As I complained, my brother scolded "If that boy liked you he would deal with me. He is some hotshot football player that is afraid of a big brother... Give it up Ali."

He was right. I was too hard to get, and the boy didn't want to try.

Now imagine another scenario. Let's jump to today, 2018. That boy is still the jock, but now we aren't sitting in the car, we are texting. He asks for a picture. Would I send it?

The answer: I think I would have hit send. Maybe not a nude, but something... Anything to get him to 'love' me. How about you? Would you have been tempted?

Spending so much time talking with teens and my children over the course of my career as a social worker/educator, I have realized some things haven't changed and never will; the desire for romance, connection, first love, and the fear of being embarrassed.

This book should do four things:
- remind you of your youth;
- give you guidelines for raising teens in a digital world;
- advise you on how to talk to your teens about their lives on- and offline;
- make you smile.

The internet has given today's teens the ease to communicate, but that doesn't mean they are having those real conversations with real people. They are still kids and just fumbling along like we were. We needed our parents, and our kids need us.

"She doesn't talk to us anymore. The only thing she cares about is her social media."

"Huh? That is all I hear as she glances up from her phone."

"Streaks, games, chatting. Even when we eat or when we are watching a movie. That kid is always looking at his phone."

"Can you not spend some quality time with your family instead of always hanging out on the internet?"

"Even when I drive my kids to school, they just sit and stare at their phones. I mean it is quiet in the car, but just not normal."

Problem: My child is always on their phone

Okay, do you remember your house phone? Maybe not all of us did this, but how many of us had a love affair with our phones? If we were one of the privileged kids, we had our own personal line and a phone in our bedroom. In my house, there were phones everywhere. There was a phone on the kitchen wall, next to my mom's bed, downstairs, and in my parents' bathroom. All of these phones had cords that extended for distances, sometimes into a different room.

When my eldest brother had his first girlfriend, he would spend hours on the phone. I would hear one of my sisters complaining, she wanted to use it too, "Get off, it's my turn to talk!"

The line was always busy at our house. My girlfriend from up the street would ring the door, "Can you play Ali, I tried to call, but one of your brothers or sisters is blocking the line. It was busy, so I just came." If it wasn't one of my siblings on the phone, it was my mom. I had the feeling she was always on the phone with her friends as I twirled in her skirts and the cord, vying for her attention.

Connecting with our friends, our boyfriends, and chatting about the silliest thing was part of our routine, "Jenny, did you see what Emma was wearing?... Mr. D. is a jerk, he stopped me in the hallway and told me my skirt was too short..." The list goes on and on. Does any of this ring a bell? I am guessing you remember the color of the phone and maybe who you spent hours talking to.

Think about it, what were you after? What did you want? You wanted to be with your peers, talk to them, connect with them, and get affirmation. "Yes, Mr. D. is a jerk."

If you ask teens today what they want when they are online they answer, "I want to know what's going on, talk to my friends, miss. If I am not on WhatsApp, Instagram, or Snap I will miss out." They want nothing more than we wanted. It is just their ways of connecting and getting the gossip, the chatter, and information have changed and we as parents have been blocked out of this... Not even able to overhear their chatter or give guidance.

What to do?

Phones out of the rooms

I hear, "I can't," or "It's too late" all the time. You can!

You pay for the phone; you are the parent. Your child might throw a fit for a few days, but if you hold your ground, it will be over soon. They will sleep better and feel happier.

My personal rule is: if my child's phone isn't in my bedroom for the night, they can't have it the next day. This only had to happen once; after that, the phone has always spent the night in my room. Set rules, set boundaries, and enforce consequences, but only ones that you can hold.

If you don't want to do this, don't say, "I can't", but rather "I choose not to deal with this." You are the master of your home, and it is fair to think something might be different for your family, but please know that you can make changes.

Set a time limit for the day

Install an app on their phone that tracks their usage. This will help them become aware of just how much time they are online and what they are using their phones for. There are several out there such as Moment or Quality Time. The newest iPhone update has this function as well. The key is to limit the time on their phones and if they don't follow the rules, take the phone away for only a day.

Talk to your child

Tell them about your day, ask about theirs, and just whatever comes to mind. Don't hesitate to talk about when you were a teen. I love teasing my dad about how he walked uphill in the snow both ways to school. He also told us stories about the 1930s and the poverty during the Great Depression. We rolled our eyes, but do you know what? Those stories stuck with me and I am glad that I know them. Some might say never talk about your youth, but I disagree. Don't preach, rather share stories of when you goofed up (especially these) and how you felt when this happened. Laugh with your kids, and ask them to explain how things work out for them; then listen.

"But they don't want to talk to me":how to talk to teens

Teens won't always want to talk to you; they certainly don't want an interview, but they need to connect with you. You need to make it easy for them. You need to be accessible. As they move around the house in the evening they may not speak to you, but they want you there. They want to hear the pitter patter of your feet and they will talk, just maybe not as much as you would like. Every child and every family is different, but there are basic moments when you can talk with great ease and without being too intrusive.

Breakfast

Eat with them without phones at the table and talk about your/their plans, politics, what is going on in the world, and send them off with a full stomach.

Dinner

Prepare dinner together and eat without the distraction of TVs, computers, or phones. Share stories about your day. This is not intrusive and is just a nice way to be together and you'll find they will start asking how your day was.

Commutes

Talking in the car is a great way of reaching your teens, but for that, you need a no-phones-in-the car-rule. This is, of course, for short commutes and not for long trips. I would use a bit of leeway on this rule. If they need to answer a message or connect the music, that is fine, but the general rule is that you are involved, "Mom, I just need to get my phone, and tell Jessica we are ten minutes late." If you are involved in what they are doing, you will not have the feeling you are cut off. The problem is not so much the phone as the lack of communication that happens with all of us the moment we enter our phone, eyes fixed upon it. One other piece of advice. Don't ask too many questions. This is not a time to interview them. "Hi, what's up?" If you get a grunt, start telling them about your day, what snack you have waiting at home, about a movie or a song. Whatever you do, no interview – just a connection, which can also be silently enjoying the same song, "Ya, I like that song too. Can you play it again? It's been a long day."

Do things together

Play video games, ping-pong, a card game, go to a sports event or another venue they might like. Figure out what they want to do and do this together. If they are addicted to their phones, sit with them and let them show you their apps, teach you a new one, and what they are doing. Learn from them. They will like the attention and the fact that you are showing interest in what they love.

Say goodnight

Stop by their room at night and say goodnight. If you stick true to the policy about no devices in the room, they just might say, "Hey you know what..." If that happens, hang out with them for a minute. If it doesn't, don't force it.

Be accessible

Whenever they come to you to talk, gauge how urgent the conversation is. If they 'really' need you at that moment you will know. If that is the case, it is time to close your computer, put your phone down, or whatever it is you're doing, and listen. If you are working and the matter is less pressing, tell them you will be done at a certain time and be there for them. The most important part is to follow through and take time for them!

"My daughter is posting pictures that are very sexy. I feel uncomfortable. What should I do? Do I forbid it? She might just create another account."

"My son follows all kinds of groups that worry me. If I talked to him about it, he would tell me I don't get it."

"My daughter told me I wasn't allowed to follow her. She has blocked me. I don't know what she is doing."

"I saw a post of some of the kids at a party. What were they thinking? Posting pictures of them drinking underage."

"Selfies, constant selfies, it drives me crazy."

"We can't even sit down for a meal at a restaurant without pictures being taken of the food. It's like she lives through the lens and not in real life."

Problem: social media

I started creating 'my brand' in the 9th grade. Just weeks before school started I went to the hairdresser, "I need people to notice me, I need to change, I want to make a statement." She smiled, "Are you sure about this?" I don't think I've ever been the same since.

I came home, walked outside to the patio where my mom was sitting and announced, "Tada! This is the new me!" I was lucky, my mom jumped up and screeched, "I love it!" I had shaved one side of my head and put a perm on the rest of my hair. She could have hated it, but she let me spread my wings.

I was purposely making a point and pushing the limits; I announced to my classmates that I was different, and I wanted to get noticed. I wore crazy outfits, mini-skirts, and branded myself as eclectic; I loved that word in the 80s. I was interviewed for the yearbook, "What's your style, Ali Thatcher?" I used only one word to answer with a confident sigh, "Eclectic." Every outfit, every look was crafted as I lay on the floor looking through fashion magazines.

We didn't have social media, we didn't have the instant pictures, but given the chance, I would have modeled myself after Elle Macpherson. She was named "The Body" after her *Sports Illustrated* swimsuit edition success. I remember posing in front of my mirror in a swimsuit trying to look like her, comparing my thighs to hers. I even remember the suit; it was a black one-piece, cut high in the leg. I moved it around and prowled on the floor trying to look just like a swimsuit model.

I wasn't alone in this self-obsession. My brother Eric loved dancing in front of the mirror with an electric guitar. He couldn't play, but he sure could pose. He would put earphones on with a Walkman and sing. We would laugh as he belted out, off-key, dancing in front of the mirror and staring at himself.

As I got older, it was less embarrassing, but my escapades continued. At an assembly at Davis High in Utah, I walked out onto the stage in a skirt that could have also been called a wide belt. This makeshift skirt I had created was matched with a piece of cloth wrapped around my chest. It was sparkling silver material; I was playing a "sexy Martian" in the sketch. From the cheers of the crowd, I had done an excellent job.

I could see the principal standing by the door at the side of the auditorium. He had his arms crossed, a scowl had spread across his face. I knew I had crossed a line.

Later that morning, I was called to his office to discuss my inappropriate clothing; the first and only time in High School I had to take that walk.

Ironically, the only time I got into such trouble was documented. There was a picture taken of me as the sexy Martian girl. Miraculously, it made it past the edits and into the yearbook.

Thinking back, had I had access to a smartphone, I might have taken some ridiculously sexy pictures. If no one had stopped me, I might even have posted them on social media. I would have looked good, too, but without any understanding of what effect my pictures might have had on others; I would not have understood how I was branding myself or what consequences there might have been. If my mom had had the chance to discuss with me the effect the pictures were having... Maybe, just maybe, I wouldn't have posted them.

I never told my mom I wanted to be in a swimsuit edition of *Sports Illustrated*; she had no idea because I was in my room with my thoughts and dreams. I just did not share these thoughts and dreams with the world. By the time I was eighteen I had transformed into a critical young woman and the thought of being 'just' an object of men's desire was horrific to me. Nobody had to know about that phase in my life. It was not online for the world to see. I didn't have emojis of eggplants (penises) and peaches (asses) posted under my pictures with

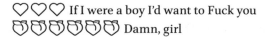
♡ ♡ ♡ If I were a boy I'd want to Fuck you
😏😏😏😏😏😏 Damn, girl

And I wasn't publicly slut-shamed. No one knew, and it was good that way.

What to do?

Follow your child on all social media accounts

Be friends with your child or follow them on everything they have. Keep up to date with what the new fad is in social media and download it. It isn't a question of whether you can or not. You demand to be their friend. Make strict rules that if you can't follow them, they can't be on it.

There are rules for you too

Do not comment on their wall, post pictures of them, or 'like' their pictures without knowing your limits. You have boundaries for them, but they will certainly have boundaries for you and you don't want to embarrass them. They are socializing here. You can be present, silently observing, but you need to give them space. Commenting should be done with their permission, privately or at home in person. If you post "Who is the cute boy?" on their wall or newsfeed, you will torture them and humiliate them in front of their entire online community, which could be hundreds of teens.

Define what you find appropriate

No one else can say what is right or wrong; that is your job. Talk to your child about your family values, what you think is inappropriate to post, what kind of language you expect from them, and for whom they are posting (is it public or for friends, who are their friends?). Every family will have differences depending on their culture and religion, but it is paramount to have a discussion with your children to clearly define the boundaries.

Spend time looking at pictures with them

Sit on the couch and discuss branding, what image on social media different kids are giving off to you vs. your child's opinions. Laugh, discuss, and critique pictures, not to be mean but to teach them your perception of what is portrayed. As you critique them, be sure to use kind language, and make sure that you yourself are not acting like teens, slut-shaming or bullying others; you're only expressing your perspective.

Spend time reading comments with them

Do this on YouTube, Instagram, WhatsApp, and on any social media you have. Learn their emoji language and ask them to explain why these comments are necessary. Talk to them about how they would feel if someone was masturbating to their pictures. For example, how would they feel about this?

"I'm going to try to 🍆💦 to your Instagram in a minute."
This was an actual message shown to me. These emojis
together mean ejaculate. The girl who received it and shared
it with me did not like this message at all. At age thirteen, she
did not share it with her parents, but she needed someone
to talk to about it. Luckily for her, her school was progres-
sive and not only brought experts in, but also gave the kids
the feeling they were there to talk about just this kind of
messaging and how to deal with it.

"I thought I would be good at this but when my son came to me and asked what a blow job was I froze."

"I expect the school to do this."

"My daughter asked me if it was okay for girls to masturbate. I never talked to my mom like that."

"I walked in to my daughter's room. She was standing in front of the mirror in her underwear, phone in hand. I yelled at her. I think I made a mistake."

"We have talked about sex, I've explained how it works, prevention, and consent but I don't get this fascination with sexting and don't know enough to talk about it."

"My son would never send a dick pic. He isn't that dumb."

Problem: Sexting, sex... I don't know how to talk about it

Think back to the introduction of this book. There I was, a teen in love with a boy, and yes, I probably would have hit send. I certainly would have sent racy messages. But what about having sex? Did I? Would I have?

I remember Homecoming, the first dance where I was in a new relationship. After the dance, we went to his house for a while, and things rapidly started getting out of control. He suggested a back rub. I said yes, but as I rolled to my tummy, he slowly unzipped my dress and unhooked my bra. I was naïve and I thought he was too. I remember thinking, "How does he know what he is doing?" as I quickly realized how fast things were moving. I didn't mind; that worried me even more.

I knew the basics, everyone did, but I was not prepared for the feelings I had. Being raised Mormon, I felt that I must be "bad" because I was certainly breaking some of the rules. I knew exactly what my parents' values were and what I could deal with and I drew the line there. I was not planning on getting pregnant. I wanted to study, to leave, and travel and I knew a pregnancy would block me. I used logic by my own device. I was strong, but what if I hadn't been? It just takes one night, one boyfriend, one date, one encounter. Sex is a natural thing and so are the emotions, but you might just want to prepare your children.

What to do?

Be realistic

This is about sex and sexting. Not all teens have sex, not all teens will send a sext. Statistics show clearly that teens today are not having more sex than we did. Nevertheless, they still are, and sexting is even more common than sex.

According to my definition of sexting and also that of The National Campaign to Prevent Unplanned Pregnancy in the US, 70% of young adults have sent a sext or received one, so don't be naïve and think "Never my child".

As you talk about sex, you need to explain how protect yourself from diseases and unwanted pregnancies. When you talk about sexting, you need to talk about safe sexting, and how not to get hurt.

Have the talk

I remember having "the talk", it was awkward, and I hated every minute of it. A long sigh with eyes rolling, "Mom, I know all about it... We're good." When I think back, she did a pretty good job. We had the talk and she was open.

My mom told me about her talk, and how she had been told her own mother didn't have one. When her mother got her period in the mid-1920's, her mom started crying and ran out of the room screeching, "My baby is all grown up."

You would think the infamous "talk" would get easier for parents, but it hasn't. Our kids are even more informed... or so we think. But the question is, do they know about the emotions, or are they just being educated by social media, pop culture, porn, the internet, and their friends with a few technical issues discussed by their school?

In a survey done in 2012 of over 4,000 young people, most said they wished they had had more information, especially from Mom or Dad, on sex and especially about relationships and the emotions of sex.[1]

With sexting, porn, Instagram, Snapchat, and the pop culture of today you need to talk to them more than ever, boys and girls alike.

How should you do this? It can be awkward, I know, but here are a few pointers.

One: start by listening to their cues
Do they ask a question while watching a movie? If yes, put it on pause and discuss it, there in front of everyone. Talk about your feelings and the emotions involved associated with whatever you're watching and then... Take a deep breath and listen to them; really listen without judging their views.

---

1   Orenstein, P. (2016). *Girls & sex: Navigating the complicated new landscape.*

Two: let your teen know you are open to talking about sex and the whole internet culture around it
Tell them that they can come and talk to you about what they are seeing and observing; that you'll take the time. Here is the trick... When they come and start talking to you, remember to put your phone, your computer, your work away and, again, listen first.

Three: find moments to connect
One of our family's big moments to connect is mealtimes. I am repeating myself here, but it is important. I will discuss anything at the table, and the kids know it. One of my daughters asked her Grandpa, "I learned in science most boys masturbate. Grandpa, have you ever done it?" I was so proud she asked, and I was even more thrilled that he answered, "Why yes, I have."

I like to go and sit on my kids' beds, tuck them in and talk. I bake cookies and hang out while they eat them, and we love listening to music on commutes. I even share newspaper articles or basic gossip I've heard, asking them for their opinion and input. The trick is... I name it as gossip if it is and I ask them what they think. I ask for their opinion. I care about what they think! Sometimes they are harsh, sometimes they get involved, but it sparks into an entirely different conversation every time.

Four: stay calm and approachable at all times
If they come to you with a question and you feel like gasping for air... Don't. Remember to stay calm no matter what the question and no matter what information is given. Do not judge or blame anyone.

Five: don't just tell them not to. It takes more than that
Whatever your beliefs are about sexual relations, you need to talk about it. I come from a Mormon background; "No sex before marriage" is how I was raised. Whatever your beliefs are, you still need to talk. Sex is everywhere, you cannot hide from it, which means teens need more than ever to have conversations (not the one-time awkward one, but rather multiple ones).

There is plenty to talk about. Here are some ideas for conversation starters: the #metoo movement, sexual harassment in the workplace or at school, their online image, sharing images, ethics and the internet, the emotions of falling in love, communication within relationships, mistakes, and of course don't forget pleasure, and this goes for girls and boys alike. Most importantly, they need to feel safe with you; you need to facilitate this feeling and these conversations.

What is safe sexting?

When approaching this subject, I think it is important to define sexting. In my work with teens and through a survey I did with young adults aged 18-30, I came to the conclusion that there are five levels of sexting.

Level 1
Written sexual messages or emojis.

Level 2
Sexy pictures fully clothed. You know, the cleavage picture or the dark and mysterious picture of a backside in tight jeans crawling onto a bed looking back ever so slightly.

Level 3
Partially nude. The ab shot with two buttons of his jeans undone like a male model, the guy's backside, jeans pulled down low showing his rear enough to give you the desire to see more, the girl in a string or half undressed teasing the camera.

Level 4
The nude. No explanation needed.

Level 5
This is video chats, FaceTime, Skype, or videos. Some teens will strip or masturbate online with others. This is home porn in my book. Make this clear to your children.

As I present the levels, I ask what can go wrong at each point. I talk about judgment, messages getting into the wrong hands, and the fact that disappearing messages don't disappear in reality. These messages can get saved and not just by a screenshot... Even Snapchat videos can be captured.

Then I let them know if they do want to send a picture, even after they understand all of the risks, please follow these rules:
- No headshots.
- No birthmarks or anything identifying it's your body.
- Make sure you can't recognize the room, the clothes, or the sheets on the bed. This is a dead giveaway.
- Be sure you can deny that it is you if something goes wrong.
- Most importantly, if something should go wrong, make sure you can live with the consequences of your entire school, your grandma, and your neighbor seeing it.

- Never forward a sext you have received from someone else to a third party. It is illegal.
- Do not videochat, Facetime, or Skype with anyone while masturbating or doing anything that would embarrass you if it was seen by others. Even if you like the person – it is dangerous, and you are putting yourself at risk.

"My son reads on his iPad at night. I trust him. He would never watch porn. Or... Would he?"

"My daughter is complaining about boys talking about sex, and porn stars in class. She doesn't want to be a snitch, but she feels uncomfortable."

"I don't know why I need a girlfriend. I get everything I need online."

"My eleven-year-old started locking his room. I checked his history and was horrified to find out he was watching porn."

"My twelve-year-old was sent a link from a classmate. 'Watch this you'll love it.' It was her first porn and she didn't know what it was. She was freaked out by it and luckily came to me."

Problem: Porn

In 1989, I was rushing to get into a sorority at the University of Utah. One of the challenges was to pick up a *Playgirl* magazine from a local magazine shop. I walked into a magazine stand at Trolley Square in SLC, Utah where I hoped no one would see me. My cheeks were flushing as I asked, "Could I please have a *Playgirl*?" The man laughed a bit, then gave me a look that made me feel dirty as he handed me the magazine. When I showed my prize possession to the sisters that night one of them pulled a nude poster of a man out and held it up in front of my face as I blushed, and everyone laughed. That was about the closest I got to porn.

You used to have to go to an XXX cinema (you know, the 18+ movie theatres located in a shady part of the city, the ones that had peep shows as well) to watch porn. I would have had no clue how to get my hands on porn in the 80s. I heard about boys who found a stash from their dad's VCRs and would watch. I knew that *Playboy* magazines were kept under the bed, but mainstream porn had not hit us and was harder to come by; still, we knew what it was.

What to do?

I repeat: No devices in the room

The rule "No devices in the room" is partially for porn. Your kids are not going to hang out in the living room to watch porn while you are sitting there. Make sure your kids use their devices in a public space.

It will happen

They will get porn sent to them or be curious and look it up and chances are at some point it will happen, they will hit click and watch some. As long as it is not a porn addiction it isn't the end of the world, it is... just porn.

Talk to them about it being just porn

They need to know that this isn't reality. You might be surprised that kids will be worried that you are just like a porn star at night with your spouse. Talk to them about the porn industry, acting, how fake it is, but most importantly talk about falling in love, sex, intimacy, and feelings.

When you just can't do this –it's awkward or you feel uncomfortable

Find a way. There is a variety of ways to do this; watch movies with them where you can easily state your views, let the school know you want a fantastic sex ed program and find out what they do, buy books and have them laying around the house, ask your GP or pediatrician for help, or even a friend who does feel comfortable to have a conversation with a group of teens.

"My daughter screams at us if we even try to talk to her about her gaming. She games all the time. We don't know what to do."

"My son attacked me when I pulled the cable out of the wall. He was screaming at me and pinned me to the wall. I was scared."

"How much is too much?"

"I am worried about what they are hearing and seeing while gaming. My son is bullied when he is playing Fortnite."

Problem: Gaming

Watching four geeky boys wearing 80s clothes in Netflix's series *Stranger Things* sent me down memory lane. My brothers used to play games in an outside shed that had been transformed into a bedroom for our oversized family. Dungeons and Dragons, Monopoly, and card games were part of their lives. They would spend hours together out there and I was jealous because I was too young at the time to enter their fantasy world. I watched in awe as they would speak of their board game adventures and which dragon they had just slain.

There was nothing alarming about them spending six hours together playing, for a simple reason: they could easily put the game on hold for a meal, they were less worried about winning, and more focused on having fun. In Dungeons and Dragons, there is no winner, the goal of these games was more to hang out together and have fun with friends.

Video games started going mainstream when I was growing up. We didn't have them at our home, but I had a girlfriend who had Pac-Man. We would sit together and watch each other play, laughing and having fun. When we got bored we would switch to jumping on the trampoline, roller skating around the block or... Yes, even playing with barbies. Barbies remained part of my life through the 6th grade.

A few years ago, I was at the home of old friends. Their teen-age son was not coming down to greet our family because he was in the middle of a game. The father of the family was visibly annoyed, but when the boy still did not come when dinner was called, our friend walked over and turned the internet off. Within a split second, there was a scream "I'm going to kill you" and thunderous steps were heard as a large teenage boy came bolting down the stairs screaming at his father. "I hate you. You ruined my game, turn it back on." He was completely oblivious to the fact that we were sitting there watching him. I knew there was a problem.

Since that time, I have seen students flunk school because of gaming, I've been called by mothers who have been physically attacked and hurt by their children, had parents break down crying being completely overwhelmed, had fathers who feel that their sons and daughters are "addicted". Often, parents complain the schools are making matters worse by introducing laptops. The kids will demand, "You can't take my laptop, I need it for homework!" The parents see them wasting time and beg for advice, "How can we stop them?"

Then I have conversations with the techies, the game advocates, and evangelists who talk about how they love gaming, about how you connect with friends across the globe, develop great motor skills, collaborate, and I have heard some professionals say "Gaming is this generation's way of socializing; let them game moms and dads!"

The last group I hear often are the parents, who comment, "I know it is bad, but they need to be popular and this is what kids do. I hope it turns out okay. My kid has it under control. My kid is a good kid, it will be fine."

This is where it becomes tricky. You can argue and debate all of the above and I will agree with elements of all of it. Gaming is fun, gaming can be social, gaming can cause addiction, gaming can help your kid to connect with peers.

What to do?

Don't panic but be honest with yourself about the risks

Be honest with yourself about the risks of gaming (addiction, age-appropriate content, violence, cyberbullying, predators, and webcams are just a few) and do not be in denial about the fact that gaming can be harmful. You are actually disrespecting those with problems if you brush this off. There is proof that gaming can be addictive, therapy centers are popping up around the globe, and the World Health Organization has named gaming a disorder.

Understand your gamer by playing with them

If your child has a favorite game, you should sit down and play it with them. Let your child be the expert and teach you about their world. You would be surprised how a kid will open up if you actually want to talk about the game they love with them. This will bring you understanding and connection.

It is not always about time, but more about how

If they are sitting with their friends in the same room gaming, laughing, eating pizza, and they are physically together,

I would not be worried about a longer game. If they are, however, alone gaming for six hours talking to a screen, I would be worried. Make sure they have time outside and with friends. Invite kids over to play.

Chores – don't make it too easy for them

Don't buy them every game, every big flat screen, every headset or gadget they want. Make them work and do chores, sports, homework, and follow the rules to earn time on their games, but also their devices.

Decide where they play

They should play in a central room in the house so that you are annoyed and will ask them to stop. Setting up what some call "man caves" and letting them turn their bedrooms into a gaming zone is inviting danger in. You will not be able to easily control their time online if you do this. I suggest no devices in bedrooms period. If you want to make exceptions it must be on request; for example, if you have guest over and want to let them game with friends in their room that is logical and acceptable.

Keep them busy

Hobbies, clubs, homework, and sports are great ways to keep them off games. There is one trick to this advice. Kids also need time to be bored and daydream, so as you keep them busy, remember not to overdo the planning and give them free time as well. Doing sports three times a week, preferably with others, and having a few social outings should be about right.

Schoolwork comes first

Make sure they do their homework and maintain their grades. If they are not maintaining what is normal for them, take the devices away.

Mealtimes and bedtimes

I know this is repetition, but it is important to remember that they need to eat and sleep to grow into healthy adults. Dinner as a family without devices, where you talk, laugh, and share stories about your day are essential. Kids should not just eat a slice of pizza in front of the game. Bedtimes are just as important, and they need their devices out of their rooms to sleep at night. They game on their phones as well so this includes getting their phones out of their rooms at night.

Make sure they have social contact with friends

This one is emotional for me because I realize there are kids who are bullied and especially these kids fall into the traps of gaming. When you talk to kids about gaming they will tell you they can be whoever they want to be in the game, creating avatars for themselves and becoming heroes. This gives some kids who are lonely and otherwise alone a sense of power and pride as they escape into these fantasy worlds. You cannot blame them, and you also cannot create friends for them. Nevertheless, social contact is important, and you will need to help them with this. It can be as simple as joining a school club, doing sports, a choir, or anything that requires them to interact with others. Let other parents and teachers know you are struggling and ask for help. You would be surprised at how many parents suffer watching their children struggle socially.

"I think my child is addicted. How do I know if they are and what do I do?"

If your child does not abide by these rules or if you are reading this realizing it is too late because they already are gaming through the night and every second they can, their grades have slipped, they are aggressive towards you or siblings, or they have dropped out of after-school activities and you are having difficulty communicating with them...

Get help! This is not something that can be easily managed on your own. Look up a gaming addiction center near you, speak to a pediatrician, or a family doctor.

If this is not an option for you, if you are skeptical of doctors and therapists or simply don't have the money to pay for it and therefore feel you must do it alone... Don't! Either find a community on- or offline such as Online Gamers Anonymous (OLGANON), or make it a family matter. Have a meeting and discuss your worries while setting up some rules. Some things that might work for you:

– A full detox. This might also be too much so be careful and know your child. Some kids will have withdrawal symptoms, such as feeling out of control, lack of motivation, emotional outbursts, loneliness, sadness, mood swings, despair, a desire to get back online, anxiety, anger, and irritability.

- Get facts and statistics and make them aware of how much they are gaming by writing it down in a log book.
- Do sports with them or maybe even hire a personal trainer that works out with them three times a week. If that personal trainer is young and likes gaming, it could be helpful because they can help you establish better behavior and they can discuss gaming while working out.
- Go on a holiday or send them to a camp that is device-free.
- Take long walks with them in nature or lay in the grass looking at the stars and talking but away from anything that reminds you what year it is.
- Know when you are implementing something like this the beginning is awful and you have to get through a few rough days.

"I saw my son has a meme Instagram feed.
It made me laugh but some of it was racist.
I am worried about his reputation."

"What is a meme?"

"I heard of those kids getting kicked
out of Harvard because of memes.
Maybe we need to be more careful."

"How can my husband and son
think that is funny?"

Problem: My child loves memes (and so do I)

A meme is a picture, image, or video that is considered humorous by many and is spread rapidly online.

It was in the early 80s and these five older brothers of mine loved peeing in the snow, making jokes, teasing me about my budding breasts, and undoing my bra as they walked by. It is a serious talent to be able to unsnap a bra through a T-shirt with two fingers; they managed this gesture with pride and gusto as I would holler and run to my mom complaining.

This wild pack of boys would generally sit at one end of a long table, huddled with my father talking and sharing their jokes. More often than not, we could overhear them. To say some of their jokes were inappropriate would be an understatement.

My mom would look sternly down at the other end of the table lined on each side with five to six kids each on any given night. "Ted, really...," she would scold as my father chuckled at my brothers' jokes. Sometimes she had to suppress her laughter as she scolded; my brothers were improper at times, but they were funny.

And then there was *MAD*. Do you remember that magazine full of comics, political satires meant to "Drive you MAD"? My brothers and father loved this little magazine and would devour the pages discussing and laughing. My mom continued to pipe into the conversation with another, "That isn't appropriate" as a conversation about right and wrong and freedom of speech erupted. This was a never-ending saga at our long dinner table. At the time, I did not understand that she was allowing us to explore our sense of humor while teaching the dangers and pitfalls. And yes, my parents played "good cop/bad cop" when it came to humor.

A few weeks ago, I was showing memes that were used in a group chat on Facebook. These memes were deemed unacceptable by Harvard and ten students who had just been accepted to Harvard had their acceptance rescinded. The students I was working with, a group of great and well-educated sixteen-year-olds, were both disgusted and roaring with laughter when they saw the memes. One of them looked panicked, "I have posted memes this offensive, miss." I sighed and said, "You are still sixteen and if it comes back to haunt you, spin a story about being naïve and not realizing what you were doing but the expiration date on not understanding this is rapidly approaching." The boy nodded and looked at me with appreciation.

I then showed them a few memes that a mother, who was also a parent coach and expert for a big national newspaper, had posted on her public Instagram account. The entire group gasped in total disgust. "That just isn't right miss. How can a mother post something like that? I would lose all respect for my mother if she posted something like that." That was precisely the moment I had them. That group of teens understood the power of posting a meme and how someone from a different generation could lose respect for you over just one post. I was doing what my mom did so successfully back then; teaching that a sense of humor is okay, but that there is a limit and some things are inappropriate and can be hurtful; you must consider how your post can be taken out of context.

To me, memes are this generation's version of *MAD magazine* or any political satire magazine that pushes the limits of what is appropriate. Think of the French and Charlie Hebdo; it is no different. These magazines exist around the world.

The difference is they have a full staff of editors considering the impact of each thing they publish; it is their job and yes, they too come under criticism and have had to live with serious consequences. They are willing to do this because they believe in their cause. This is not the case with teens and thus it requires the guardians and parents to sit down and teach them.

What to do?

Keep your cool

If you realize your teen is posting troubling memes, approach the subject calmly and openly. Remain non-judgmental and ask them to explain and put the meme into context. If it makes sense, which it might easily do, explain how it could hurt them if someone else saw this or took a screenshot of it.

Look at memes with them and have a laugh

You might be shocked that they find things you think are funny inappropriate. It is eye-opening to share memes you see with them and ask them what they think. Ask them to share some of their favorites and discuss and then maybe go old-school, take a trip to a comic book store.

Peer pressure online is real

Remember that your teen might feel a lot of peer pressure to be posting memes on a group to be "cool" or enter a group. They might be following inappropriate groups that some "popular kids" have created in a bid to up their social standing. Be understanding if they have made a mistake and teach them how to deal with this by following the sound advice on the next page.

Give them this sound advice

Teach them to consider before posting or sending a meme. If they believe the meme could possibly cause them harm or be misunderstood but they still want to share it with their friends tell them:

1 Do not post or send a very offensive meme to anyone! Not even a best friend.
2 Look at such memes in person with your friends – I repeat *do not send or post*!
3 If someone asks you to forward an offensive meme simply explain to them what they need to google or which website to go to if they want to look at it.

"I got a bunch of Sarahah messages that really hurt. The worst was: 'ur a little triehard with a huge ass nose u skanky bitchh.' It really hurts. Why would someone send that?"
Girl, 13 years old

"I had an Instagram account made about me. The sole purpose was to humiliate me."
Boy, 16 years old

"It isn't possible to get away from bullies. Every one of us has seen it."
Girl, 15 years old

"I don't want to tell my parents. It will just make them worry and if I tell the school it will get worse, but I am not feeling good. Really... I am so sad but can't describe it, I need help."
Boy, 12 years old

"I don't bully. I'm just kidding when I say those kinds of things. Kids our age get it when you call them a loser, an idiot, or an annoying fuck online. They know it's a joke."
Boy, 13 years old

Problem: Bullying

Snow had been falling all night and there was a layer of snow and ice on the sidewalks. The school janitor was working on clearing the path, but it was impossible to keep up with the amount that was coming down. As a nerdy 9th grader, I was walking to a class in an annex and had to pass these slippery sidewalks.

I was still awkward and my social skills hadn't kicked in. I had been tripped daily for weeks by a group of bullies. They were the popular girls with big poofy eighties hair, glossy lipstick, and confidence that I did not have. They were jeering me as I stared at my books, head bowed, hoping nothing would happen. They misjudged the ice and snow as they gave me a little shove to send my books flying. They got more than they bargained for: as I fell forward, there was a loud snapping sound and I was sure the bone was broken. I sat in the back of the classroom, tears trickling down my cheek as the blood drained from my face. A nice and brave girl raised her hand. "Excuse me, I think Ali had her arm broken. Can I take her to the office?" The bullies remained silent as I was walked to the office.

The principal knew I was being bullied. He had not succeeded in stopping it and now he wanted names. He was angry. I begged the school not to make the call to the parents of the other girls. The principal was a wise man and didn't listen. He made the call.

Those parents got the call you never want to get. They were informed, "Your child broke a girl's arm at school, she has been bullying."

Now a mother myself, I imagine the mother sitting there in shock, ashamed, disappointed, and hurt thinking:

"I have raised you to never hurt someone else, how could this happen?"

There was a punishment, discussion, tears, an apology and, after all of this, promises that it would not happen again.

Let's take a step back and look at this scenario. Without that phone call, the parents would have lived in complete innocence, assuming their child was the angel they raised her to be. The call is hard to make but essential.

This was the last time I was bullied at school. These girls graduated with me and they were even friendly towards me over the years that followed. One call from a brave principal, parents that listened and cared and the problem was solved.

Today, you have not only this kind of bullying but also online bullying. This means kids can be bullied when they are home, in the one place that is meant to be safe for them. For a bullied child it is as if they cannot get away from it. When I went home in the 80s I was safe, nothing happened, and I could forget about my bullies, not worrying that my phone would chirp announcing another mean message, image, or remark.

So, what to do...
for on- and offline bullies

Have the passwords of your child's devices

Some children would never tell their parents they are being bullied; they are ashamed and do not want to burden their parents. It is your job to be able to go in and look for clues if your child is acting strange or sad.

If the bullying happens online

Do not answer the bullies and collect the proof. Take screenshots and ask your child to do so as well. Explain that if they shoot back rude remarks it will look bad for them as well and they need to stay cool.

Inform the parents of the bully for on- and offline bullying

Get the school involved. If it happens at school, they should be bold enough to make the call for you, and it is their job.

What to do if the school refuses:
- Ask the school why they are refusing and listen to their response.

- Get your facts straight, calm down, sleep on it and get as much information as you can.
- Engage other parents. See if other children are being bullied or have witnessed it.
- If you find an ally or a friend that is willing, have them drop the bomb for you. It is much easier to have a third party say over a coffee, "Hey..., I've been hearing rumors that your child is bullying... Do you know about this?" That little nudge should send any parent into research mode, and discussion mode. The bully will be aware he is being watched and will hopefully step back.
- Rally friends of your child to help; online and in class. Talk to the parents of your child's friends.
- Don't cry wolf. Try to teach your kid to deal with one-off bad behavior and save that call for the real bullies.
- If all else fails and you are sure you aren't wrong, make the call! Make sure you are calm and open-minded. Approach the parent in a respectful way, asking how you, together, could solve the problem your children are having.

If you get the call and it is your child bullying

Listen to the parent calling and stay calm. It is hard to make the call and the person calling you is possibly very angry and in pain. Take the call seriously and know that your child is not perfect and there must be some truth to the call. Do not excuse them or defend them – rather, figure out the problem, resolve the problem, possibly punish them and have them apologize.

I've always liked the saying about it taking a village to raise a child. To stop bullying, it certainly does; you need kids, parents, teachers, and administrators to all take a stand.

Teach them how to deal with group chats

Maybe your child didn't know how to share as a preschooler; you taught them. Chatting online and certainly on a group is no different. It is a skill. You need to understand when to be silent, when to write, and how to calm a toxic situation.

When I ask teens to raise their hands if they have seen someone getting virtually beaten up on a chat every hand in the room shoots up. Every teen and tween has either been a victim, done the beating up, or been a bystander.

Chats and comments can be horrible to deal with not only for teens, but also for adults. If someone is bullying on a group, confronting them on this group will do no good. As many teens have told me, "This just makes everything even more toxic, miss." I agree.

I teach teens first to help the person who is getting beaten up online by sending them a private message. "Hey, I see what's happening. I like you, and I am sorry." This will help the person immensely and is just a pure act of kindness. Tell your kids not just to be a bystander but to send that private message.

The next step is to stop the bully. Tell teens that if a friend or someone they know well is bullying or acting out of line, call them. Tell the bully calmly why they could get in trouble and ask them to stop. If you can't call, send a voice message.

Voice messages are always better than a text as texts can be misunderstood and you don't want to start a fight. Chances are that kid might have just flunked a test or gotten in a fight and is feeling pretty miserable. A misunderstood or condescending text could make things much worse.

Encourage your kids to come to you for advice and help if they feel they can't do anything, and they know the situation is out of control. Remember to take screenshots if someone is being bullied.

Their digital footprint

The first day of high school my history teacher was calling
attendance: "Thatcher, Ali". He looked up over his glasses,
"So, I have another Thatcher... Are you anything like your
siblings? Would you be more like Aaron or Geoff or maybe
even sweet Rachel? She was quiet, you look like you might
be trouble, Thatcher. I am going to call you Thatcher from
now on!" He moved to the next child as I sunk in my seat
with frustration. That particular teacher never called me by
my given name. I was forever just one of the Thatcher clan;
forever fighting for people to see me as just me.

Five older brothers and four older sisters meant the walls
of Davis High were whispering about our recent escapades;
one brother got kicked out, another broke into the school
to steal tests, almost all were fierce debaters.

When a storm blew in with vicious East winds, the power
went out in the middle of the school day. Students were
told to stay put, but, inevitably, some students did not obey;
dark corners of the school were found as dramas and love
stories unfolded. One of my sisters liked a boy. The two of
them decided this would be the perfect moment to make
out in a corner. Nobody could see as they found a protected
and secluded area in the hallways. The kissing was rather
intense when the lights went on and they were so involved
they did not immediately stop; not until there was laughter
and an uproar; fingers pointing their way as they pulled
apart.

That afternoon my mom heard urgent hollering as the front
door was pushed open, "You will never believe what... did at
school. She is in so much trouble. I am soooo embarrassed...
How could she?"

I was living in the footsteps of my sisters and brothers. These stories have long faded and disappeared. Nothing unusual happened. We were teens, we were stupid occasionally, we fought, and we embarrassed each other.

If that same scene had happened today, ten phones would be pulled out of pockets and bags. Some teens would film as yet others would post, and within seconds this story would be part of the world wide web for millions to possibly discover; it would not vanish, could always be found, and blown entirely out of proportion and context.

I lived in the footsteps of my brothers and sisters and when I fell in love with a German man who wanted to sweep me away to Europe; nothing sounded dreamier; I ditched everything to start a new life abroad. I had a chance to recreate myself. Ironically, I spend time talking about my beloved family and sharing our stories. The difference is that I choose to tell them and can spin them the way I want. I was able to get away from being "a Thatcher from Farmington" and just be me.

Today, teens not only have to live in the footsteps of their parents and siblings, but also in their own digital footprints. They are doing this while they and those around them naïvely stumble along, many without control, creating their own digital footprint.

My mother used to look up over her book when we were going out, "Remember your name! You will be representing all of us tonight!" Sometimes these words haunted me at a party, and yes I held back on occasion because I did not want to let my family down. Today, you might need to add,

"Remember your name before you post something because you will possibly hurt not only yourself but others and your family as well if you make a mistake."

What to do?

Awareness is everything

Young digital natives claim to know everything about the digital world, but trust me, they don't, and it isn't always easy for any of us to keep up. Read about online safety, if the school has an evening go and, better yet, demand (in a polite way) that the school inform you annually on the newest online trends for teens. Talk to your teens and tweens about what you are learning and listen to what they have to say. They might teach you a thing or two as well.

Keep track

Keep a list of all accounts you make, all of your email addresses, and delete the accounts you no longer use. Do not just forget about things and leave them lurking on the internet for years. Teach your kids to do the same thing and make sure you keep it clean.

Google yourself

My son laughs when he sees me do this. Every month I google myself, and I ask my kids to do the same. My eldest daughter changed her privacy settings once she saw what came up when she googled herself. I google people all the time and seriously, if you are nineteen and applying for an internship, would you want a silly 5th-grade video of you to show up? I googled someone who wanted to work with me recently, and precisely this happened. I was forgiving and laughed at the video, but someone else might be less understanding.

Don't overshare and watch out that your kids don't

All this fuss about what teens post... What about you? Clean up your chats, your posts, and don't overshare. Think before you post. Do you really want to share that? Does everyone need to see? I left a fitness group where we had to post sweaty selfies to encourage each other to workout when a colleague mentioned my posts were hysterical. I looked at her in shock, "The group is private!" Her answer, "I am part of it but don't exercise... I have fun watching you all."

I do post a fair amount, but each time I post I do it as if the whole world is watching.

Teach your kids to do this and to think this way as well.

Searching is also visible so watch what you search

If you are on your computer and ads pop up for something strange ask yourself who was on this device before you? The algorithms are targeting you, using cookies and sharing your information. Remember you are saying something about yourself when you search.

Digital tools exist, so use them

Of course, there are tools to monitor your children, and you might want to use tools to help them make good choices and block dangerous sites and content, but there are also other helpful applications to keep you private and make your life and your teens easier. From password keepers to VPNs and different blocking applications, you can use the internet and its tools to keep you safe and private. My favorite application and the one that has helped me the most is called Moment. It tracks how many times you pick up your phone, when and how long your pick ups are. Apple decided to add this as a function in their newest update as ethical design becomes important to developers. Follow websites and blogs to keep up to date on the newest tools or ask your children's school for tips on the best tools. Remember rule number one: Awareness is everything.

The Golden Rule and the Grandma Rule

If you follow the Golden Rule, you'll never really go wrong. Who can argue with the words "Do unto others as you would have them do unto you"? Too often we just assume kids think about this; it needs to be discussed, and posts need to be analyzed together. Not only your children, but also you would do well to follow this timeless rule.

So, what is the Grandma Rule? I was using it before I read that YouTube also uses this term in their teen safety section. Before posting, think of how you would deal with your grandma seeing this post. Families, values, and cultures can be different. Who am I to say what is right or wrong, but if you cringe thinking of your grandma, parent, or future bosses seeing it, don't post it.

Creating change: When you've done it all wrong and you're like uh-oh

My brother was eleven and I was ten. He was a year behind in school, which meant he was in my grade. Having a brother in the same grade, sharing friends and teachers is a bit tricky as you head into adolescence. I didn't see it that way at first, to me it was a grand adventure. The biggest adventure of all was the fact that I had met my brother just days before, at the Salt Lake Airport Terminal One, "Ali, this is Eric, your new brother." This isn't the usual way to meet your sibling; a hug, a smile, and some awkward emotions.

Each of the five times my parents decided to adopt, they held a family meeting. They explained their intentions, and we could voice our opinions about the upcoming adoption. We felt that we were involved in the process and prepared for that first day at the airport. Each time my parents took this bold step, our family changed. Some changes were small, others more significant; less travel, less hiking as someone wasn't capable, fights, laughter, bedroom changes, sometimes embarrassment and always a sense that we were different.

I have had my own bouts with change as an adult. International moves, learning foreign languages, and then there was a change we have all been confronted with: changes in technology.

When I got my first iPhone in September 2009, I was overjoyed. I was so proud of this new device. Laying it on the table at a restaurant was like showing I belonged to the elite smartphone clan; I was hip, reachable, connected and up to date. My husband had his BlackBerry, and as the children grew up, each eventually received an iPhone. The change came gradually. At first, I used my phone primarily to connect with friends and family and it was cooler than anything else.

Then I started downloading more apps, reading on my phone in the parking lot of the school, using it for my calendar, my guide, and compass. My husband and children were no different; before you knew it we were changing, and I didn't mind, I loved my phone.

As phones continued to update, so did I. I learned new things, enjoyed new tricks, and acquired new skills. My phone was my alarm clock, my way of connecting, working; essentially an extension of my arm and my brain, ever present. It was great that my children could always reach me, and I could always reach them. I was becoming a different kind of mother, and then, all of the sudden, my rules started changing, and as they did I felt less connected to my children regardless of the fact that I was tethered to them via my iPhone. I noticed I had slipped. Slipped too far. It was a slow, creeping change and as good as some of it has been, I think many of us might need to adjust, rethink, regroup.

I know the moment I lost control was during an international move. We moved, the family was off balance and a new status quo crept into our lives without me wanting it to happen. It was 100% organic in the coming; one morning I woke up and realized I had ditched some of my values along the way. There I was watching my son; he did not converse with me anymore. Not in the car or at home. He was always on his devices, non-stop and when I asked him to put his phone or computer down, he either got angry or looked up bored, "I am busy doing homework." I knew I had to do something.

My first thought was, "Oh boy, this is going to be ugly." I knew that forcing change upon a teen or anyone for that matter is disrupting the status quo. My son was happy with the situation, his lovely smartphone and his apps, podcasts, streaks and online connections; or at least he thought he was.

My mom told me once, changing something in a family is just like tugging on a mobile above a baby's bed; as you add a new piece to it everything else becomes unbalanced. The other objects will search for a new place and swing around violently; chaos is set into motion. You can watch this happen but eventually, the mobile will slow down, find its balance, and everything will fall into a new order as the mobile will sway ever so slightly as a breeze comes through the window of the baby's room.

Many things can cause a family unit to get out of sync; a new baby, adopting a child, a child leaving for university, divorce, and yes, even the introduction of smartphones and new devices; anything that changes the way we function and communicate will disrupt the way things are.

I remembered my mom and her parenting before going to my son to have the talk. She had to change the way in which she dealt with one of my brothers. He was in trouble all the time, and their relationship wasn't great. She saw a therapist, and he asked her, "How badly do you want to change this?"

She replied, "I really want to. I have to."

"Good, because I will tell you one truth. You need to want this change because he doesn't want it and if you force it, things will get worse before they get better! I can help you, but *it will get worse first.*"

My mom gasped, "Worse? I don't know if I can do worse?"

"I repeat. Chaos and anger will come if you implement new rules; it will get worse before it gets better."

He was right. It got worse as my brother resisted the change. My mom and dad stuck to it and they now have a beautiful relationship with that brother. Change and a new status quo found its way into their relationship.

When I put the new tech rules into place and reminded my son he couldn't have a phone in his room, I first apologized that I had slipped. I explained why I had slipped. He sat there scowling and you would have thought the world was coming to an end as I wrapped up. He was tense and angry, "Mom, I am the only kid who won't have their phone all the time. My friends will all think you are evil. You are so old-fashioned; you don't get anything about our generation! Tssss. You know I hate you sometimes?" He squirmed in his chair and revolted against me saying some pretty nasty things. We discussed this a while longer, he knew it was hopeless, but he might gain some traction. He finally asked to have his phone on Friday and Saturday nights, "I need to practice self-control Mom; I am getting older. If I follow your rules during the week will you allow that?" I did.

It took about a week of minor arguments for the complaints to reduce. I don't hear arguing anymore. On a rare occasion, he will smile as he plugs in his phone at night, "You know you are an evil, strict mom?" I answer, "I know, I love you too." His long arms swing as he smiles and heads to bed. Sometimes I follow him to his room and sit at the edge of his bed talking to him. He would never admit it, but he sleeps better, his grades have improved, and he doesn't really mind. The rule is simple; his phone has to be in my room by the time I go to bed, if I ask him to put it down he must obey and if he doesn't, the phone is confiscated for 24 hours. I only had to do that once.

It only took about a month for us to move past the stage of integration and find a new norm and it was well worth his anger towards me.

What to do?

Be honest

If you want to change but don't have the force to endure the chaos, it might not be the right time and you might want to stick with the status quo. Don't lose your reputation and be a pushover to your kids by starting something you don't believe in or feel you cannot do. It is your home and if the rules you have are working, you are happy enough, and don't want chaos, you don't have to change because you read a book, or someone tells you to. If, however, you are in pain, are frustrated with your kids and want to get phones or gaming devices out of the rooms, away from the dinner table, and reduce the time online, be honest about how difficult it will be.

Know the stages of change and tackle them with gusto

Virginia Satir,[2] an American 20th-century family therapist, created steps of change within a family unit. It is so much easier to handle the chaos if you understand the changes and can follow them as they happen. Satir's steps are the following:

2   Satir, V., Banmen, J., Gerber, J., & Gomori, M. (1991). *The Satir model: Family therapy and beyond.*

1. Late Status Quo – This is your research stage. Seek improvement and information from the outside.
2. Resistance – Your kids and possibly your spouse will give you this. Rather than blame them, help them to open up, become aware, and overcome the reaction to resist and deny.
3. Chaos – There are no magical solutions. You cannot have change without a bit of chaos. You need to build a safe environment, acknowledge the feelings of frustration, possibly your teen's fear of missing out (FOMO). Stay with it, stay strict, and then the magical next stage starts to happen.
4. Integration – I find discussing new solutions, new times to use devices, new ways of communication, and talking about how teens feel when they are digitally disconnected helps. They might not admit it right away, especially if they are mad at you, but the integration of these rules brings relief, and the last phase settles in.
5. New Status Quo – This will stay intact until you realize you need change or until a new device or system has thrown everything off again.

Involve your kids

As parents, own some of the problems and take responsibility for your part if you, too, have done something wrong. Talk about why you think change is necessary. If you can get your teens on board with your ideas, the change will be smoother. If you simply walk into their room while your child is gaming or mindlessly sending a thousand streaks on Snapchat, ignoring your demand to set the table and you scream, "That's it. There are new rules and from now on you will...", they will revolt. This really isn't the best approach, even though that snap of anger gets the best of us.

It is better to take note of what is happening, make a strategy, prepare yourself for the talk, sit down with your spouse and your children and explain what needs to change and why. Your kids might shock you stating, "You think I am bad, you also need to change, like really, you chat all the time with your girlfriends, and live on Facebook. Dad is always checking his emails, sports results and the news non-stop. Seriously!!! You think you want me to change? Look at yourself!" This would be a good time to stay calm and discuss and set new rules together, for the entire family. As you enforce these rules you will get some resistance, even if everyone agreed because it caused disruption and chaos. Stick with it even if it is tough.

If your kids decide they don't want to work with you on this, know that you can still enforce new rules. It will just be harder, but remember you are the parent and you can do this if you want to badly enough.

Modeling: and what about you?

As a child and teen, I focused on what my parents didn't do for me. I would honk the horn in a parking lot because I wanted to go home, and Mom was chatting with a girlfriend, I pulled on her skirt, stood in front of her when she talked and complained about anytime that was not meant for me. My dad came under my criticism too. I had no understanding for the fact that when he had left for work at 5:00 a.m. and came back at 5:30 p.m., all he really wanted to do was read the newspaper, eat, and decompress. I wanted his attention and I wanted it NOW. I did not understand, how could I? I was too young.

For years, I took for granted the sacrifices my mom and dad made. To me, everything they did was normal. I did not appreciate the late nights, my mom standing behind me holding my hair while I was ill, the times she sat with me until 1:00 a.m. talking about boys and life even though I know my dad was waiting for her, she was tired and yes, I was only one of the eleven children she did this for.

My mother and my father did one other thing for me that I have only come to value recently. They set a good example; no, let me correct myself: a great example.

Being from a religious family, I was surrounded by many adults who were striving to be their best, to be kind, and to set an outstanding example. As I left home and my religion and moved across the world, I have changed, tried new things, and had grand adventures. One thing has never changed: being a role model for my children and the students I work with is an important part of my life. From my clothing, my gestures (as simple as holding a door), to my language, and the way I treat others, I strive to set an excellent example, hopefully showing understanding, kindness, and thought. Sure, I goof up; my mom did as well, but we have one thing in common. We are aware of the importance of being a good role model, and we try.

Today, parents have a new challenge: we need to be online role models. How we use our devices, how much time we spend in front of the screen, what we post, the way we write online, our pictures – all of this will influence our children, how they think of us, and the way they will behave online and interact with their much-loved phones and computers.

For work, I scour the internet to understand the online behavior of teens. This work has branched out to parents as I realized you cannot separate the two. In almost every workshop with teens, I show posts by adults, otherwise respectable adults who have crossed a line online. The disgust from the teens is stronger than my own. I hear them gasp in shock that an adult could post something so rude or crude. "Is this a private profile, miss? Please tell me this mom isn't public." One kid said, "I would break my mom's phone if she posted things like this." I inform them that this adult clearly forgot that she wasn't in her living room with five girlfriends giggling, but rather online with 800 plus followers and an open profile.

The next stunning realization was when asking teens to monitor their time online, there is a sigh that always collectively goes through the room, "Why don't you talk to my mom? She spends hours on Candy Crush and seriously I can't hear her complaints about my time."

"My mom is addicted to Facebook. When I am talking to her she doesn't look up from her phone. Really she can't tell me what to do. I wish she would put her phone away."

"My dad checks his e-mails and news at the table. Eye contact with him? Never at the table. He would never listen to you, miss."

From a four-year-old, I heard, "Mommy is always on her phone!"

Unfortunately, the current political climate is not helping things. Rude tweets and attacks. Stress at work and the need and desire to be connected to our friends. One young millennial mom of three I often talk to said, "Don't tell me not to use my phone; it is my connection to my friends, my lifeline, and my sanity. I need you to offer support and empowerment instead of criticism. Unless YOU are going to help me watch my child YOU should not be critical of the way I do it."

I get it. It is hard and lonely. Look at my mom; she got honked at, I know she cried, I know my parents were stressed, and I know they talked to their friends and colleagues and needed connection, and quite frankly I have always needed it too. It is, however, our role, as parents, to talk about what we see; but most importantly we need to set the example. If we want our kids to connect in a healthy manner, we need to study ourselves before we have these conversations with them.

What to do?
(this is the peace offering to that millennial mom friend of mine)

Analyze what you are really doing with your phone

Take note for a week or two of what you are doing online. Download an app like Moment or Quality Time and track yourself. Some of the newer phones might even have this function. The newest iPhone update has it built in. It is easy to track how much time and how you are spending your time online. Be honest with yourself.

Block some of your apps

You can go into your battery settings and see how much you are using your phone for certain apps. If you are spending too much time on a certain app, a game, or social media block them after a certain amount of daily time. There are apps to help you manage your time online. Don't only use them for your kids but for yourself as well.

Don't phub your kids

A phub is when you are snubbed by someone with a phone. You know the feeling, you are talking to them and they start looking at the phone, "Ya, uh huh, that's right." You could tell them a meteorite is headed for their head and they would just continue, "Ya, uh huh." If you are out with your kids for quality time, turn your notifications off or the sound down low, and put your phone in your bag. That ping will get you to pick up your phone in the middle of a conversation you are having with your child. Don't! They deserve your attention!

Close your devices when you talk your kids

When my kids want to talk to me and I am writing or working in front of the computer, I will sometimes immediately close my computer or put my phone away. Other times I will tell them that I am busy and ask if they could wait a moment. It is essential to close down electric devices when having conversations with your children.

Establish no phone times for you and your kids

It is your choice when and how, but analyze your behavior, listen to what your children and your spouse are saying to you, and find times when you don't need/use your phone. I have mentioned no phones at the table, leave them away when you are watching a movie, reading stories, and maybe even when you are out and about.

Read a book or a magazine – and not on your phone

When you go to the park, read on the couch, or even in bed, read paper, not electronics. Kids know when you are reading a book or a magazine and will never complain. If you spend your time reading the news online, they might not understand and will see it simply as time online and away from them. They will attack you that you are playing Candy Crush or chatting with a friend and be honest: if the phone pings and you are reading the paper, you will switch to chat with your friend. We are all guilty of this.

Watch your behavior in meetings and lectures

Are you constantly checking your emails, your messages, the news? If you are, you are probably just like your teen and most likely not performing as well as you could. In a meeting, be present – turn the phone off. If you need it for an emergency for a child or a boss who might call, there are settings for this. You can set your phone so that you can only be disturbed by certain people. Use your phone to protect yourself.

Talk to your friends on the phone rather than chatting

It is much healthier for kids to hear you talking than to see you chatting. When you are chatting with a girlfriend, your children can't see what you are doing. If they hear you laughing hysterically after a friend tells a joke or a funny story they will look up from what they are doing, "What did she say, Mommy?" They will want in on the chat because it is real. If they can hear you talking they know who you are talking to, they feel like they are part of it, they hear the emotion and, especially for small children, they are learning language skills.

Communication is impoverished by chatting; it is so much nicer to talk so just be bold and call. I find when I call people they seem surprised, "Why are you calling? Is there a problem?" I always say, "Nothing is wrong, I just prefer talking." Even though speaking on the phone makes multitasking harder, it is worth it: Actual spoken conversation is the richer form of communication... Try it and you will see.

Set up healthy habits

I have some habits that have helped me be more balanced. I follow the same rules I ask my kids to follow. I have a real alarm clock, we charge our phones out of the room, I don't check my phone first thing in the morning (my seventeen-year-old can't quite manage this... He hides in the bathroom on his phone), I go to yoga and run without my phone, and I simply turn it off sometimes. I also have a home phone number. I know this is strange and old-fashioned and it is hardly used but if someone really needs me, they can call that number, even at 2:00 a.m. I will pick up. This way I don't feel like I am cutting myself off when I turn my phone to silent. If someone needs me, they can reach me. If you find this too strange, buy a second cell phone as a home phone. Just get a sim card and use it as a phone only to call with, with the most basic settings. The people who "need you" 24/7, be it family or your boss, can have this number.

Follow these kindness rules when you post

Before you write on a group chat or post ask yourself these
three questions:
   Is it honest?
   Is it kind?
   Is it necessary?

How many times have I seen a snarky remark, an inappropriate picture, or a dig online and this from adults? This would
not happen as often if we took the time to reflect.

Once mastered, teach this to your kids. Ask them to ask
themselves these questions and tell them you do. If you have
not been kind in the past: clean it up and tell your children
how you, too, had to change and work on yourself. They will
like hearing about your blunders as well and it will make it
easier for them to open up about their own.

Go vintage

Long and lanky, my seventeen-year-old accompanied by his fifteen-year-old sister charged into my room the other night with a smile spread across his face as he carried a stack of photo albums. "Want to look at old pictures Mama?" We sat for at least an hour laughing, turning pages, and telling stories.

When I was a little girl, we put old jeans on and headed up a creek. The water was streaming at a fast rate, and we found just the right spot to slide. Moss had grown over an old cement viaduct that ended in a pool. I have never forgotten this day, or the times we played Uno, Cluedo, and Monopoly together, the water fights, the laughter.

Technology is upon us, but kids still like some of this old-fashioned stuff. Bake cookies, make jam, go berry picking, play board games, listen to music, go window shopping, do a jigsaw puzzle, play ball or throw a frisbee in the park.

Getting the computer and phone out of my son's room caused some havoc and chaos, not only because he couldn't chat and check social media non-stop, but also because he loved listening to music. I had two ideas to help: wireless speakers, or vinyl records. He decided he was willing to try. The speakers were not his favorite option. We went to a record store in Amsterdam. The girl working in the shop was young, blond, hip, kind, and explained everything about the joy of going vinyl. I think we were in the store for at least an hour. My son has since become addicted, upgraded his system once already, spending hours going into the store and looking at the latest vinyl. The store offered him a job; he listens non-stop as I will hear the music blaring out of his room. It drives me crazy sometimes, but I know his style of music, I know he is reading or relaxing and as I pop my head in, I see him on a chair reading the New Yorker and listening to David Bowie. This passion would never have developed without me being strict. He loves his vintage attitude, and so do I.

It doesn't have to be a vinyl hobby; it can be anything from having water balloon fights to shooting some hoops. Find a way to connect with your kids with no devices or old-fashioned ones, and some magic will happen. You will still have a phone and so will they, social media will still stay a part of their life but connecting without it to nature, to others, to their soul will create a new awareness and pleasure.

Some other ideas of vintage activities

Go to the library

A library is quiet, full of books and magazines, and it is an excellent way to connect with peace and books. Children and even teens can find great pleasure in going and even just be flipping through magazines or comics. You would be surprised at what you can find in a good library.

Go outside

Anything from having a picnic, a bonfire, skiing, going to the beach, a walk or a hike. Wherever you live, take the time to enjoy nature with your children. I love lying on the trampoline and looking at the stars talking and laughing. It doesn't have to be complicated but get out. Find a ping-pong table and have a go.

Play cards or board games

A few weeks ago, I was playing poker with some teens. I loved it. It was a first for me. It doesn't matter what the game is, just play. It is a great way to talk, connect, and just be together without the distraction of a screen.

Cook and bake together

There is nothing better than eating cake batter. I have two kids who love cooking and baking with me and another who only enjoys eating what we make. Nevertheless, all three of us end up in the kitchen eating the dough, talking, and laughing.

There are so many ideas, and every family is different. I can coax and nudge, but you need to find your own passion, your own way of connecting. It might even be photography and developing black-and-whites, but figure out a way to spend offline time together. Connect, talk, laugh, and share and feel how much more balanced you are when you take a break with your kids.

Final thoughts

That day in the car, an 80s song took me back in time. My heart was pounding, and my thoughts were racing as I realized I had never asked myself the question, "how I would have behaved if I had had a device?" I was horrified by my honest answer and I realized this might be just the link many parents need... To think back and ask themselves, "What kind of teen was I? Would I have?"

Ali, the 80s girl with a crush on a football player, has grown up. As a teen, I fell in love, fell out of love, made mistakes, learned about friendship, love, responsibility, and values. The conversations and open dialogues I had at home, with friends, and teachers, were key to me surviving my teen years and in making me into the person I am today.

That's right – conversation and open dialogue with your teens about their lives on- and offline is the key to helping them be good digital citizens and grow up into responsible, happy, loving adults. It doesn't matter if the conversation is while walking a dog, eating dinner, jogging, or washing the dishes. What does matter is that you are having these conversations, and often.

The basics of parenting haven't changed, we have just been a bit distracted lately. We need to remind ourselves to close the screens and look up from our phones when talking to our kids.

I am not planning on giving up my smartphone anytime soon. I love having an encyclopedia in my pocket. I don't ever want to give up the internet and all I have gained from this great invention.

No, I don't want to go back to the 80s, I just want to get back to some good hearty conversations and see fewer kids making mistakes and getting hurt.

My son still argues when I am strict, "Mom, you just think phones are bad!" I don't, and he knows this, just as he knows that I love him and his sisters; but hey, he is a teen and loves to push my buttons.

Acknowledgments

Without the hundreds of hours spent with teens, parents, and teachers, I would never have been able to write this book. Thanks to all of you who have shared your stories, your Instagram feeds, your insights, and sometimes your pain with me. I cannot do my work without you.

A special thanks to Camilla Hannuksela and Mascha Koopmans Portier for your hours of comments and proofreading. Thanks also to Sanne Bloemink for introducing me to Marjolijn Voogel at AUP, who believed in this book and has guided me through the process. Lastly, a warm thank you to the very talented Ricardo Rivera and Corinne Guy for the artwork and the cover.

About the author

Allison Ochs is an American/Swiss social worker, lecturer, teacher, and consultant. She has been married to a charming German man for almost thirty years, and they have three children. When she is not on the road sharing stories with teens, parents, and teachers to help them navigate and live in harmony with their smartphones and various devices, you will find her either in Amsterdam or a picturesque town just above Lake Geneva.

By Mickelle Bench Weber

@Allison Ochs